Self-Esteem

The Indispensable Guide Brimming With Confidential Insights On Bolstering Self-Assurance In Various Everyday Contexts

(A Comprehensive Manual For Enhancing Self-Compassion And Elevating Self-Esteem)

Chester Schaefer

TABLE OF CONTENT

Introduction 1

Leadership And Extroversion 7

Advantages Of Enhancing Self-Esteem And Self-Assurance 32

Strategies For Cultivating Motivation Towards Goal Attainment 42

Understanding The Roots Of Self-Esteem: Exploring The Sources Of Personal Emotions 51

Consistent Self-Improvement Is Paramount In Achieving Success. 73

Tools For Self-Awareness 136

Introduction

Life has the ability to leave you utterly disoriented and overwhelmed. Throughout the process of maturation, guardians aspire for their children to cultivate self-reliance and assurance. However, regrettably, this parental aspiration often induces in offspring a sense of inadequacy in meeting the expectations set forth by their parents. Furthermore, the scope of the matter extends beyond that. Navigating through the intricate web of interpersonal connections, the lingering wounds inflicted by acts of deceit or emotional distress can significantly erode one's self-assurance to a great extent. You placed your trust in life, only to be bitterly let down. Nonetheless, you are not solitary. Numerous individuals globally encounter comparable challenges, which manifest in diverse manners. - Certain individuals may exhibit a negative response, while others may display resilience and recover swiftly. - There may be individuals who retreat in response, whereas others bounce back resiliently. Based on the observation that you are perusing the contents concealed within the cover of this book, it is discernible that you are endeavoring to emancipate yourself from the state of despondency arising from a negative self-perception. There is no need for you to experience any negative emotions irrespective of prior events that may have occurred in your personal history. The rationale behind your behavior is rooted in your choice to bring the burdens from your prior experiences into the present, thereby cultivating a regretful inclination to dwell on the past.

One's self-esteem can suffer significant harm throughout the span of their life. One believes they have achieved a state of organization and stability, only to have their foundation abruptly disrupted, causing their reality to become radically disrupted. One might be taken aback by the considerable number of individuals who harbor negative feelings toward themselves. This phenomenon is intricately related to the manner in which they have been subjected to treatment by others, as well as their own interpretation and internalization of such treatment. To acquire self-assurance, one must set aside all of those concerns, which is undeniably a significant challenge. Nevertheless, there are actions that can be taken to enhance one's self-acceptance, embracing all imperfections, and ultimately achieving personal success, which is a fundamental right afforded to every individual globally.

This book was authored as a consequence of collaborating with individuals who display a deficiency in self-assurance and observing their subsequent personal growth and development. I presumed that by disseminating these compelling instances and outlining methods to cultivate self-assurance, it was plausible that a contingent of contented readers would derive benefits from the book. The book caters to individuals of all backgrounds who possess self-awareness or struggle with self-assurance, offering a comprehensive guide towards building and cultivating a robust sense of confidence. You will be required to undertake specific tasks that have been substantiated to enhance levels of self-assurance. Consequently, by the culmination of the book, you should experience an improved sense of self and a heightened ability to project yourself positively to the world.

Furthermore, you will gain insight into the profound impact of self-esteem on each of your interpersonal connections, and comprehend the reasons behind its potential to diminish the overall satisfaction and fulfillment of your existence. If one's expectations fall short of recognizing the inherent entitlements of every individual, one shall not attain beyond those limitations. Nevertheless, should you alter your beliefs and develop a positive self-perception, you possess an equal capacity as anyone else to acquire the self-assurance requisite for navigating through life with greater satisfaction.

Leadership And Extroversion

Numerous prominent and accomplished individuals have demonstrated that introverts possess the potential to excel in leadership roles. In addition to the aforementioned individuals mentioned within this literary work, it is worth noting that other well-known figures with introverted tendencies include Abraham Lincoln, Eleanor Roosevelt, Charles Darwin, and Steven Spielberg. Individuals who possess audacity and vitality frequently have the inclination to assume prominent positions and demonstrate self-assuredness while conveying their ideas. However, it should be noted that this does not automatically equate to being an efficacious leader.

Given the organizational framework and the specific nature of enterprises, there are certain businesses where individuals with introverted tendencies may not find themselves ideally suited. Nevertheless, the perspective held by the majority that extroverts are superior to their more reserved counterparts is misguided. The attributes inherent to each individual are crucial in establishing a harmonious organization. Rather than engaging in a dispute over superior leadership, it would be advantageous for both parties to seek common ground through making concessions and collaborating harmoniously. Nevertheless, the enduring social stigma surrounding introverts necessitates the emphasis placed on identifying their shared characteristics with effective leadership. There is a prevailing belief that introverts lack the necessary vocal talents of extroverts to effectively lead, inspire, and propel their subordinates forward. That is indeed one favorable aspect of these reserved individuals - their astuteness enables them to diverge from customary practices and attain comparable, and occasionally superior, outcomes.

Characteristics of Introversion that Contribute to Effective Leadership

1. Good Listeners.

Extroverts display a linear thought process, as elucidated previously, as they adhere to a collectively sanctioned predetermined framework of guidelines and protocols. Their responses and choices are governed by this factor, which poses a challenge to their willingness to embrace novel concepts on a frequent basis. In contrast, introverts attentively listen to suggestions and meticulously contemplate these ideas.

However, compatibility continues to be a significant factor in the group's overall effectiveness and efficiency. Based on the findings of a study conducted by Francesca Gino, an associate professor at Harvard School of Business, it has been observed that teams where leaders exhibit introverted traits and subordinates are proactive tend to achieve remarkable success. Similarly, supervisors who dominate conversations are more compatible with compliant employees who prefer direct instructions.

2. Ability to Focus.

The contemporary era in which we live is replete with numerous sources of diversion, making it arduous to focus one's attention on a specific task or endeavor. Due to their inherent proclivity for solitude, introverts exhibit a willingness to embrace the absence of external stimuli and delve into the profundity of their own thoughts without trepidation. Engaging in intellectual contemplation enhances their cognitive faculties and refines their capacity to concentrate.

During meetings, introverted superiors often assume a reserved demeanor, appearing unconcerned and disinterested, yet in reality, they meticulously assimilate all the information being presented. One remarkable aspect is that they engage not only in the absorption of information, but also in the simultaneous initiation of theorizing, imagining, and planning.

Issues are occasionally subject to discussion in the workplace, leading to a common tendency for individuals to be diverted by the evident matters. It is often these subdued yet influential individuals who tend to identify the solutions owing to their ability to concentrate on the matter at hand and approach it from various perspectives.

3. Humble.

Jane T. In 2006, a study was conducted by Wadell of Regent University pertaining to the concept of Servant Leadership. Her research unearthed remarkable findings. She discovered that there is considerable overlap between the esteemed characteristics of Servant Leadership and the inherent attributes of introverted individuals, and one of these shared traits is humility.

The characteristic that sets this style of leadership apart is its commitment to fostering the personal development of followers. Individuals who possess these administrative qualities abstain from actively seeking attention and are not motivated by ego-driven pursuits. They hold the belief that by fostering the growth of their followers' abilities, they attain the utmost potential of their organization.

4. Mild Tempered.

As previously stated, individuals who exhibit extroverted tendencies often have a tendency to vocalize their thoughts. Thus, they will articulate their current emotions regardless of their nature. Occasionally, an issue arises when individuals are confronted with stress-inducing circumstances, as these situations can evoke highly adverse emotional responses. Furthermore, this can be attributed to the fact that the energy they expend is derived from their surrounding environment. Consequently, if the atmosphere is replete with warmth, they will assimilate it and manifest identical behavior.

However, their counterparts in the polar regions tend to display a calm and composed demeanor. In the midst of disarray, an introverted leader possesses the ability to instill discipline and tranquility within a turbulent workplace by bestowing upon it their own composed presence. This attribute often goes unnoticed by a significant number of individuals and is occasionally regarded as a disadvantage. Nevertheless, it holds the potential to serve as the most formidable advantage for an individual who leans towards introversion. You possess a commendable capacity to remain composed despite the captivating nature of the unfolding events. Indeed, you may possess the capability to alter these occurrences through the projection of the appropriate energy.

5. Creates Meaningful Connections.

In the context of conferences, it becomes discernible which individuals exhibit extroverted traits. They are individuals who possess an excess amount of energy, often seen engaging in constant movement from one seat to another, engaging in conversations with various individuals. Indeed, while extroverts may amass a greater quantity of calling cards, it remains uncertain how many of those encountered individuals will retain any recollection of the interaction.

In contrast, their counterparts tend to restrict their interactions to a select few individuals; however, in doing so, they cultivate a profound connection.

It is frequently observed that individuals aspiring for career advancement must establish a robust professional network. The primary consideration in this pursuit is to establish connections with as many pertinent individuals as possible. However, the essential aspect that holds true significance lies in fostering strong relationships between the individual and their network. While it is conceivable that you are acquainted with Mr. CEO due to a brief conversation, it is important to note that acquaintanceship does not guarantee friendship. In order to appropriately classify the nature of your relationship, you and Mr. CEO can be considered acquaintances rather than anything more substantial. And it is best to avoid being relegated to the acquaintance-zone, as his recollection of your visage, let alone your name, would be exceedingly faint.

Overcoming Introverted Tendencies for Enhanced Leadership Skills

Within every inherent strength lies a corresponding weakness. Indeed, there are certain benefits that come with being an introvert in both professional and personal spheres. Notwithstanding, there will inherently exist certain characteristics intended to counterbalance your seemingly superhuman attributes. Frequently, however, an individual tends to devote excessive attention to these aspects, overshadowing the positive ones.

Reiterating their nature can assist you in harnessing these characteristics and allowing your introverted strengths to manifest themselves.

1. Leave your comfort zone.

Introverts typically exhibit a preference for solitary work as it aligns with their optimal functioning. Their cognitive abilities are fully optimized, and their innovative capacity is enhanced, hence solitude provides them with solace. Nonetheless, effective leadership necessitates ongoing engagement with one's subordinates. Engaging in self-exposure may present challenges and discomfort, yet it is imperative for one's growth as a leader. It is not sufficient to depend solely on one's cognitive abilities. Success also takes teamwork.

2. Speak your thoughts.
Occasionally, introverted individuals become engrossed in contemplation to the extent that they neglect verbal communication. The concepts you propose may prove challenging to articulate due to their potential for excessive complexity, yet nonetheless, it remains imperative to convey them. In a tumultuous corporate environment, these strategies may present the remedy that the leadership has been seeking. Moreover, amidst widespread panic, you possess the rare ability to maintain composure, enabling focused analysis of the situation and articulate discourse unlike anyone else.

3.4 Exercise Caution in Verbal Communication

Exercise caution and reflection before uttering words, or abstain from speaking altogether. This is a matter that necessitates your personal resolution. Certain individuals require additional attention to one aspect, while others would benefit from focusing on the alternative. The majority of individuals are capable of establishing equilibrium within their lives. What is the desired equilibrium that is being discussed in this context? It lies in the delicate balance between demonstrating kindness and maintaining unwavering honesty. The aforementioned pair of factors should be your primary objectives when it comes to your communication efforts. Occasionally, there is an intersection between them, while at other times, there is no convergence. An individual who consistently adheres to honesty may not invariably exhibit kindness, and an individual who exhibits kindness may not invariably display absolute honesty.

When discussing the concept of honesty and stating that it is "not always completely" applicable, we are referring to the fact that its universal application does not encompass all situations. Typically, dishonesty is not the most optimal solution. However, it is acceptable to make a decision to provide an answer that refuses to engage with the question.

Individuals who possess adeptness in expressing their thoughts may appear somewhat eccentric to our perception. They appear to hold extreme perspectives as they have relinquished all inhibitions in expressing themselves, unabashedly voicing their opinions while exhibiting unwavering boldness in their interaction with the world. Frequently, these individuals are the ones articulating thoughts that align with our own or embody the qualities we aspire to possess. These individuals frequently embody eccentricity, encompassing both the countercultural enthusiasts, the romantics, and the creatives who can be found in public spaces.

Those individuals who fail to consider their words before expressing them will reveal their entire selves to you. They will elucidate the true essence of their statements, providing you with a comprehensive understanding of their intentions, and enabling you to ascertain their character. It is an indisputable reality that embracing openness inherently exposes one to vulnerability. Instead of fearing this reality, you have the opportunity to wholeheartedly accept it. Gandhi was reputed for his unwavering stance on the principle of nonviolence. In the event that someone were to seek to assail him, he would permit their attempts without reciprocating resistance. In this instance, you are providing a clean canvas upon which humanity can inscribe acts of malevolence. The notion posited was that an individual's complete adherence to nonviolence would render them a symbol of the malevolent actions of a wicked individual, serving as a paradigm for all of humankind. By undertaking this action, we are appealing to the fundamental essence of what is morally favorable for the betterment of humanity. By undertaking this action, we are embodying the sacrificial embodiment of benevolence, conveying to a malevolent individual our willingness to surrender our existence rather than succumbing to their demands of retaliation. It is evident that this represents the ultimate scenario, namely the prospect of perishing due to expressing one's opinions. Nevertheless, there is much to be gained from studying Gandhi's philosophy of nonviolence, even amidst acts of hostility.

Occasionally, an individual's endeavor in their personal growth entails exercising greater deliberation before verbalizing their thoughts. This pertains to the core of integrity, namely the axis of benevolence. Integrity should be consistently balanced with compassion. This is attributed to the fact that they are two fundamental principles of great significance.

4.3 Forgiveness

Indulging in a victim mentality is a regrettable pitfall that we have all succumbed to at some juncture in our existence. It is necessary to adopt a different rhythm in order to decelerate and introspect on the underlying reasons for one's thought process. By possessing a profound understanding and a commanding ability, one can both regulate and comprehend these conditions. Perceiving oneself as a victim can be justified at times; undoubtedly, there are instances when we find ourselves in the position of being victims. From a certain standpoint, each of us is subject to the consequences imposed by the environment in which we exist. We are brought into a societal construct that imposes stringent demands upon us. The majority of families exert influence on their children to conform to a particular lifestyle. In contemporary American society, it is primarily anticipated that individuals will attain a college degree and initiate a family. This in itself does not constitute a significant misconception, however, when coupled with additional societal demands such as those based on religion or material wealth, it can induce unwarranted anxiety in individuals. They indeed fall prey to the systemic challenges.

Can you conceive of alternate scenarios in which individuals are authentically subjected to victimization by the system? There are many examples. Racism exemplifies systemic victimization, leaving those affected with no recourse but to confront their condition of being victims. The phenomenon of structural racism within the United States manifests in the disproportionate representation of individuals from racial minorities within the prison system, the spatial segregation of these communities, and the implementation of laws that subject individuals from these groups to prosecution to such an extent that their lives are profoundly impacted. The ratio will vary among individuals based on the extent to which bigotry has impacted their lives. However, this specific instance provides a distinct illustration of the current state of victimhood among humans: certain individuals have already experienced victimization.

An additional classification pertains to the working class or those in a state of financial disadvantage. This specific demographic is systematically hindered from engaging in specific sectors of income within society, resulting in significantly limited access to goods and services compared to individuals belonging to the middle or upper social classes. This serves as an additional illustration of how certain individuals are compelled to confront the societal constructs that have influenced the condition of their lives.

There is hope, however. Regardless of their circumstances or the hardships they face, every individual should have the opportunity to discover hope and overcome adversity. The innate inclination to seek solace and regain one's emotional equilibrium is an inherent trait of human nature. It is crucial to grant oneself the freedom to navigate through life's inequitable impositions of societal norms and expectations in a manner that aligns with personal conviction.

May I inquire as to the methodology you employed for accomplishing this task? To commence, it would be prudent to recognize the formidable powers that suppress you. I acknowledge that I have experienced systematic oppression due to my impoverished upbringing, yet I am determined to leverage my personal agency in order to transform my circumstances. An individual assuming the role of a victim might express, "The circumstances of my life have been perpetually unfavorable, which is lamentably unsatisfactory." "I hereby resign." Although it is true that the world is unfair, the latter part of this statement is inaccurate.

The matter at hand pertains to the inequitable nature of our world. The world is inherently unpredictable and unforgiving, as evidenced by the extensive expanses of untouched wilderness that exist devoid of human presence. There is a complete absence of any form of organization in these locations, aside from the innate arrangement dictated by the natural laws governing the earth. Entropy is prominently evident in these locations, namely the rainforests, swamps, vast deserts, and enigmatic oceans. These are the locations where we witness the truly adverse circumstances that life is subjected to by the world. In order to persist, it is imperative to possess the capacity to safeguard oneself physically against the perils existing in the world. One's existence is contingent upon the establishment of one's own realm of being. While you are entitled to proceed accordingly, it is imperative to note that the endeavor may prove arduous. Within the realm of nature, no aiding hand exists, nor are there any human observers to bear witness to the dispensation of justice. Individuals who possess weak physical constitutions, are of tender age, or advanced in years, frequently succumb to mortality.

Nevertheless, humans possess an inherent duality that compels us towards self-improvement, justice, and ethical actions. This enables us to discern between moral correctness and incorrectness, and undoubtedly, there is a significant presence of malevolence in the world. Hence, it is imperative to recognize that although humans possess the capability and inherent inclination towards benevolence, a considerable number of individuals deviate and engage in malevolent behaviors. We are unable to place complete and profound trust in the entirety of humanity. It is imperative that we exercise discernment in placing our trust, and prioritize our own well-being.

Taking personal responsibility is an invaluable attribute to possess, while avoiding a victim mentality. An individual who has been victimized lacks the means to advocate for their own interests and regain functionality. They have fallen prey to unfortunate circumstances, succumbed to their own volition, and resigned themselves to the challenges of existence.

There are compelling justifications for abstaining from assuming the victim role, one being that it is devoid of enjoyment. The situation lacks a significant narrative progression. The individual in question becomes the recipient of criminal actions, thereafter assuming the role of expressing lamentation and portraying themselves as a vulnerable individual afflicted by their circumstances, incapable of self-remedy. You should reconsider assuming that particular role. Our preferences often shape the roles we assume in life, and if it does not align with your true nature, it would be best not to adopt the victim mindset.

The individual lacks a fundamental sense of identity. Numerous individuals experience traumatic events, from which they subsequently evolve, acquire knowledge, and advance in their personal growth. Individuals possess the capacity to effectively navigate traumatic events and assimilate a wide range of life experiences into the fabric of their overarching psyche. They allowed their traumatic experiences to resolve and become a distant memory, granting themselves a state of tranquility, choosing to refrain from dwelling on their past adversity, except when necessary to engage in a healthy process of mourning.

Nevertheless, certain individuals develop an emotional bond with their sorrow. They cling to it as if it were an enduring narrative they desire to be part of indefinitely, thus becoming the narrative that defines their entire life. It is disheartening to witness as frequently individuals find themselves compelled to persist with such circumstances right from the outset, without any alternative means of escape.

Nevertheless, while navigating through such experiences and grappling with the ensuing trauma, individuals inevitably endure harm to specific facets of their self-perception, ultimately failing to acquire effective means to reverse said harm. These individuals consistently revisit their challenging experiences or traumas in their minds, and they are unable to fully recover from them. They perceive themselves as individuals affected by cancer, individuals who have experienced depression, or individuals with alcoholic parents, and this begins to shape their self-perception.

This is the problem. One's identity cannot be established by embracing negative notions. The experiences of enduring cancer and facing mistreatment on one occasion alone should not constitute the sole emotional baggage you bear. Think about it. If that is the underlying belief that you are subconsciously affirming repeatedly, contemplate the implications it has on your perception of yourself. This implies that you consistently reside in proximity to mortality, or rather, that your consciousness perceives a concern. This lifestyle is profoundly unsatisfactory, and an individual must wholeheartedly assimilate in order to achieve genuine advancement in their self-actualization. An individual who exhibits a perpetual unwillingness to overcome obstacles and advance further in their endeavors will be intentionally evading the discomfort of personal development. However, in the process, they will inadvertently subject themselves to significant hardships and anguish in the future.

Advantages Of Enhancing Self-Esteem And Self-Assurance

By this juncture in the book, you have acquired knowledge concerning the adverse consequences stemming from low self-esteem as well as its prevalent origins. Now, we shall proceed with acquainting ourselves with the advantages associated with augmenting one's self-esteem and self-confidence. As previously stated, self-esteem and self-confidence are interdependent and mutually influenced. Lacking a strong sense of self-worth, it becomes exceedingly arduous to cultivate the necessary self-assurance needed to accomplish the objectives one aspires to fulfill throughout their lifetime. By acquiring knowledge regarding the advantages that stem from possessing a robust sense of self-worth, individuals may initiate their drive and engage in the implementation of strategies designed to enhance self-esteem. Keep in mind that even though it is harder to increase self-esteem later on in life, it is not a lost cause. Similar to the majority of endeavors in life, it necessitates diligent effort and dedication towards other significant aspects, namely self-awareness and self-acceptance. If you are an individual who currently has young children or is contemplating having children, it is important to bear in mind that the development of self-esteem is highly susceptible to influences during the formative years of a child's growth. Take into consideration the environment you are fostering for your children, and bear in mind the significance of instilling a sense of worth and dignity in them. By instilling in them an ample measure of self-esteem as their foundation, they can develop into individuals who possess unwavering confidence in their own capabilities and aspirations. Firstly, let us commence by garnering knowledge regarding the invaluable advantages associated with cultivating a robust sense of healthy self-esteem. Subsequently, we shall proceed to the exploration of the merits linked to the development of self-confidence.

Advantages of Enhancing Self-Regard

Listed below are five advantages that accompany the augmentation of self-esteem:

• The development of self-esteem enhances one's ability to assert themselves.

• Self-assurance enhances your assertiveness in making decisions.

• The cultivation of self-esteem fosters a sense of emotional well-being, promoting feelings of trust, confidence, and authenticity within interpersonal connections.

• An individual's self-esteem diminishes the probability of remaining in a detrimental relationship.

- Self-esteem facilitates the cultivation of pragmatic outlooks on oneself as well as others.

- The cultivation of self-esteem enhances an individual's ability to withstand and overcome stress and adversity.

Enhancing Self-Esteem Enhances Assertiveness

The ability to express oneself confidently and honestly is an indispensable skill that individuals must possess in order to maintain equilibrium in their lives. When an individual possesses self-esteem, it greatly aids them in fostering a robust confidence in their verbal expressions, actions, and inquiries. If an individual holds the belief that they desire or require something, it becomes unnecessary for them to devote time contemplating the opinions of others regarding its veracity. Individuals who possess a limited sense of self-worth encounter difficulties in exhibiting assertiveness due to their apprehension of potential scrutiny or rejection. They hold the belief that requesting something represents a display of vulnerability, and as a result, anticipate being negatively evaluated for expressing their needs. Contrarily, an individual possessing a robust sense of self-worth does not harbor apprehension regarding articulating their needs, as they are devoid of any uncertainty in this regard. Self-esteem is derived from holding affection and admiration towards oneself, thereby enabling individuals who possess this sense of self-care to experience a strong sense of normalcy when expressing their desires and fulfilling their needs.

To further elaborate on the concept of assertiveness, I will offer a straightforward illustration. Envision a scenario where your mother entreats you to promptly come to her residence in order to assist her in packing and relocating her belongings, in anticipation of her imminent move. Nevertheless, given the challenging week you have endured at your workplace, it was already part of your agenda to allocate your evening engaging in leisurely pursuits, such as indulging in a film viewing and partaking in a soothing bath." In this particular context, assertiveness entails the capacity to uphold and prioritize one's own needs in parallel to those of others, including one's mother. In this scenario, an individual possessing a robust sense of self-worth would express, "I am deserving of this respite as it is necessary for my well-being." Conversely, an individual harboring low self-esteem might convey, "It would be self-indulgent of me to partake in an evening of relaxation while someone seeks my assistance." An integral aspect of self-esteem lies in recognizing the fundamental truth that one cannot provide assistance or support when their own reserves are depleted. In this particular scenario, assuming that the individual possesses diminished self-regard, there is a high likelihood that they will earnestly attend to assisting their mother in the process of relocation, notwithstanding their profound fatigue. Consequently, the aftermath may evoke a sentiment of diminished regard for their personal temporal boundaries by others. Nonetheless, one cannot gauge another's sentiments without effective communication, hence the mother should not be held responsible for merely requesting assistance.

Presented herein is an additional illustration of assertiveness. This instance shall pertain to the professional environment. Consider the scenario where, on multiple occasions this month, your supervisor has requested for your assistance in completing your colleague's report, as they have consistently failed to meet their deadlines. It is evident that your boss is well aware of your superior productivity in comparison to your co-worker. An individual with sound levels of self-esteem would express, "This marks the third instance within this month where I have been approached to assume additional responsibilities, owing to John's recurring delays." I place a significant emphasis on being a collaborative team member; however, I experience heightened levels of stress and overwhelm when consistently tasked with additional responsibilities. "What measures can we implement to prevent a recurrence of this issue?" This is the preferred approach to address your supervisor, as it demonstrates assertiveness and communicates that you do not tolerate being consistently exploited, ensuring you maintain your self-respect. An individual with diminished self-esteem in this particular scenario would probably acquiesce to assume the additional workload, ultimately harboring feelings of resentment towards their colleague as a result. It is probable that they will excessively exert themselves as a result of the additional workload, leading to attributing blame on others and ultimately cultivating detrimental interpersonal connections. By engaging in effective dialogue and expressing your emotions, you afford others the opportunity to gain insight into your perspective and make appropriate modifications to their behavior.

Acquiring the ability to assert oneself is an essential life skill that holds significant importance, given its frequent utilization and widespread regard. If an individual believes they are afflicted with the "yes" syndrome, the initial course of action they might consider undertaking is to address their self-esteem, so as to cultivate an ability to acknowledge and honor their own desires and requirements. Please bear in mind that assertiveness should not be confused with aggression. Assertiveness involves maintaining a resolute and unequivocal stance regarding one's needs and desires, whereas aggression pertains to an insistent and forceful approach. The manner in which an individual articulates their message, employing nuances in vocal inflection and nonverbal cues, significantly shapes the manner in which others perceive the appeal being made.

Strategies For Cultivating Motivation Towards Goal Attainment

Motivation denotes a trajectory that is set in motion by a rationale or objective. It is crucial to comprehend this aspect: the presence of a rationale and objective serves to stimulate motivation.

For instance, it proves to be challenging to make progress towards a goal when one lacks a discernible rationale or objective. In essence, you require a foundational framework or compelling rationale for the commitment of effort, in order to generate momentum and facilitate progress from your current state.

If you possess a strong inclination to engage in a particular activity, it is highly probable that you will experience motivation to pursue it. Therefore, there is no need to exert conscious effort; your desire alone will suffice to propel you into action. It is important to bear in mind that there may exist valid reasons and purposes for lacking motivation, which could result in a lack of drive to take action.

Certain individuals define motivation to be a compulsion or an aspiration. Alternative phrasing in a formal tone: "Motivation, according to different perspectives, is commonly delineated as the exertion of effort in one's professional endeavors." To me, motivation holds no significance. Motivation is indeed the force that resides beneath the impetus, aspiration, and labor. It is this intangible force that influences the caliber of an individual's drive, intentions, and the effectiveness of the subsequent action-reaction interplay stemming from motivation.

Furthermore, this innate drive, referred to as motivation, arises from the extent to which an individual is living a life infused with purpose and in harmony with their authentic self and heartfelt desires.

Personally, I perceive motivation as a form of energy that encompasses physical, mental, emotional, and spiritual dimensions. This energy can be described at one extreme of a continuum as positive, succulent, robust, dynamic, venturesome, thrilling, indulgent, curative, etc., and at the opposite extreme as inert, obstructed, sullen, motionless, despondent, adverse, destructive, etc.

Motivation is a cognitive and physiological phenomenon, primarily rooted in bodily processes. Based on my observations, it is uncommon for individuals to explicitly state "I think I'm motivated." Instead, they often express their motivation as a feeling, such as "I feel motivated," or conversely, "I don't feel very motivated."

Furthermore, expressions such as "having a strong desire", "lacking enthusiasm", "instinctual reaction", and "physical limitations hindering mental determination" among others, which revolve around the abdominal region, also indicate the body as the primary source of motivation (in contrast to the mind). This region serves as the focal point for the energy that propels individuals towards action and sustains their state of motivation. Motivation, in my personal experience, is an intangible feeling.

So, in my perspective, everyone possesses motivation, albeit potentially not aligned with the preferences of others or even the choices we ourselves would consciously opt for.

So,

When I engage in internet browsing, rather than directing my attention solely to the task at hand, I find myself driven.

I am driven when I perceive employees as functional entities rather than individuals.

When I am inclined to engage in gossip, bullying, and sarcasm when communicating rather than speaking respectfully, lovingly, and compassionately, I am driven by a particular motivation.

When I opt to compromise integrity in my business practices and succumb to avarice instead of adhering to ethical principles, I am motivated.

When I decide to perceive conflict and negotiation in terms of win-lose rather than win-win, it serves as a source of motivation for me.

When I opt to engage in fraudulent tax practices and deviate from my dietary regime, I am driven by motivation.

When I opt to allocate only 75% of my energy and effort towards my work, as opposed to fully committing at 100%, I am driven.

I find motivation when I opt for dishonesty, deceit, and theft instead of adhering to principles of honesty, integrity, and trust.

When I opt to display childlike emotional behavior instead of exhibiting emotional intelligence, I am compelled.

When I permit my ego to obstruct my path, engaging in actions that undermine my progress, rather than operating from my true and genuine nature, I am driven.

When I opt to tune out in front of the television, rather than zealously immersing myself in my tasks, I am driven by a sense of motivation.

When I opt to engage in an extramarital relationship instead of investing effort in my current partnership, I am driven by motivation.

When I opt for hatred instead of love, I am driven by motivation.

So, everyone is motivated.

Once more, from my perspective, the crux lies in the caliber of the impetus's energy and, furthermore, the substructure on which the quality of said energy rests.

The factor that underlies the caliber of the energy I allude to as motivation is purpose.

In my perspective, purpose is driven by the heart, in contrast to being driven by the intellect or ego. Intent can be considered as the essential factor that imparts significance to our existence. Once more, I would assert that motivation is intrinsically linked to both purpose and significance for me.

The distinction between purpose driven by the heart and purpose driven by the ego is what determines individuals' literal and figurative location in the continuum between having a clear purpose and lacking purpose, as well as between finding meaning and experiencing meaninglessness in their professional, personal, and recreational pursuits.

In many instances of our existence, we progress from undertaking an action to attaining the corresponding outcome, repeatedly transitioning from one action to its subsequent result. The inquiry at hand pertains to the factors that motivate my actions. The underlying factors that fuel the motivation (energy) behind my actions. The trajectory of an individual's life is frequently evaluated based on this dynamic, and many also assess 'success' by considering the transition from action to outcome.

In the broader context, personally, the vigor and caliber of the cause-effect relationship and the level of commitment to achieving 'success' are contingent upon leading a purpose-driven life and determining the origin of one's purpose (whether it stems from ego or the heart).

Understanding The Roots Of Self-Esteem: Exploring The Sources Of Personal Emotions

To engender an improvement in self-perception, it is imperative to undertake an earnest examination of the underlying causes contributing to one's dearth of confidence or the harboring of negative self-perceptions. Investigate thoroughly as it is highly probable that the solutions lie within the following:

Parental disapproval

Enduring interpersonal connections that deteriorate

Facing accusations for various matters

Assuming responsibility for situations that have occurred

Criticism originates from various sources, often emerging during the formative years of one's development. Have your parents communicated their sense of disappointment to you? Did you experience feelings of unattractiveness in comparison to your peers? Did you experience any instances of being subjected to ridicule or taunting from others? Did you experience disappointment from an individual who held the responsibility of loving you?

It is imperative that you reflect upon your life and ascertain the origins of the negativity, as without acknowledging its source, your ability to conquer it shall remain limited. In the event that your parents, for instance, instilled negative feelings within you regarding your identity, it is imperative to comprehend that such sentiments represent their subjective viewpoint. Each individual holds their own set of opinions, yet when these opinions are projected onto others, it reveals a deficiency within themselves rather than providing an accurate representation of one's identity. In instances where parents encounter difficulties, it is often observed that they tend to resort to placing blame. "I have not raised you in such a manner," or "Considering all the efforts I have invested in your upbringing." The reality is that parents occasionally instill guilt within their children due to their lack of experience in parenting, leading them to mistakenly attribute blame to the child instead of their own parental abilities. It is necessary to document the root cause of the negativity and externalize it through written form.

Exercise in understanding

It is evident that our self-esteem is influenced by the individuals in our surrounding environment. Please make a note of the individuals who had an impact on you and record the content of their statements. It would be advisable for you to observe the inherent frivolousness of the situation. For instance, if an acquaintance were to express that you exhibit a lack of emotional stability and did so in a derogatory manner, it would not contribute positively to your self-perception. Please record the identity of the individual who inflicted pain or expressed disapproval towards you, and subsequently detail the nature of the criticism received. We are taking steps forward from today onwards; therefore, considering this documentation, it will be the final occasion where you are subjected to encountering these troublesome entities. It is commendable to thoroughly investigate the origin of the negativity, as doing so enables a proactive approach to precluding its recurrence in subsequent endeavors.

Look at your list. Comprehend the information and subsequently shred it into diminutive fragments. Those individuals in your vicinity who engendered negative emotions within you lack the authority to do so. As you carefully dismantle the written words, contemplate the vanishing of negative emotions, for they solely endure as such while you grant them permission to persist. Today marks the commencement of a fresh chapter in your life in which you shall confidently embrace the world while being content with your authentic self. Today, it is expected that you will adopt an optimistic mindset towards your own personal characteristics, with the intention of progressively cultivating formidable self-worth and genuinely embracing your authentic self throughout the duration of this literature.

Determine which individuals in your social circle exhibit toxic behaviors. These individuals are characterized as exploiting your resources or bringing negativity to your life while offering minimal reciprocation in exchange. They are the individuals whom one hesitates to contact, as one is aware that they have a tendency to exploit others without offering any reciprocation. You do not possess a predilection for appeasing others. Cease reclining and allowing yourself to be the object of someone else's exploitation. Identify your genuine companions and allocate a greater portion of your time to them, while minimizing interactions with individuals who seek to exploit your willingness. Acquire the ability to decline requests and do not experience remorse for doing so.

In the subsequent chapter, we shall examine the manner in which the mechanics of existence are observed through the lens of equity. Based on this analysis, it will become apparent how to level the playing field. Inequitable circumstances are an undeniable reality, and if one experiences a dearth of self-assurance or self-assuredness, it becomes imperative to ascertain the appropriate measures to alter one's perception of life.

Negative Self-Esteem
Insufficient self-esteem can give rise to diminished self-appreciation, leading to self-defeating attitudes, cognitive disempowerment, social challenges, or

harmful behaviors. This perception holds significance, as there is a compelling case to examine self-esteem not solely as a cause, but also as a consequence of problematic behavior. As an example, in a certain lens, children may develop a detrimental self-image, consequently giving rise to feelings of despondency. On the other hand, experiencing discouragement or an absence of proficient functioning can lead to negative emotions, thereby potentially diminishing one's self-esteem.

Adverse self-perception is further noted to be a perilous determinant, culminating in mental derangement and even captivity. When individuals possess a deficiency of self-confidence, they find themselves ill-equipped to effectively address routine challenges, resulting in a diminished ability to reach their maximum potential. This has the potential to result in a decline in both physical and mental well-being. A decline in emotional well-being may result in the manifestation of maladaptive behaviors, such as depression, anxiety, and eating disorders.

Individuals displaying high levels of self-esteem tend to consistently attribute positive occurrences to their own abilities and characteristics on a global scale, while attributing negative circumstances to external factors. This tendency reinforces and reinforces their positive self-perception. Individuals with diminished self-esteem tended to attribute negative events to stable internal factors and global factors, while attributing positive events to external factors and chance.

In the context of longitudinal studies, the identification of low self-esteem during childhood, pre-adulthood, and early adulthood has emerged as an influential predictor of subsequent unhappiness in later stages of life. In the comprehensive analysis of relapse, it was evident that out of the last two factors, namely social support and self-esteem, only self-esteem exhibited a significant correlation with severe feelings of despondency.

The predominant significance of self-esteem during the schooling period is systematically examined in studies pertaining to eating disorders. During this particular stage of existence, the elements of weight, body form, and the monitoring of caloric intake interweave with one's individuality. Researchers have identified diminished self-worth as a precipitating factor in the emergence of eating disorders among female adolescent students.

Low self-esteem also seems to be wary of the unfavorable outcome of intervention in such a matter. The significant influence of self-esteem on one's self-perception has led to the implementation of programs that employ the cultivation of self-esteem as a cornerstone preventive measure for eating disorders. In conclusion, there exists a consistent correlation between self-esteem and the assimilation of problematic behavior. Moreover, there is ample empirical evidence to suggest that low self-esteem may contribute to the erosion of inclusive behavior, whereas the enhancement of self-esteem could prevent such deterioration.

Though the rationales behind such practices vary and are difficult to anticipate, a multitude of scientists have acknowledged the significance of self-esteem in the prevention of misconduct, rehabilitation, and societal transformation. It is noteworthy that both diminished self-confidence and inflated self-confidence share a connection with the amplification of unsettling manifestations.

Having a lack of confidence and a tendency to be pessimistic can impede one's ability to embrace responsibility and constructive feedback, thereby hindering access to opportunities and deterring one from embracing new challenges, consequently depriving them of fulfilling experiences in life. It can also result in the dissolution of important relationships. The occurrence of low self-esteem can stem from various factors, exerting a profound impact on our emotions, perspectives, behaviors, as well as shaping our self-perception and interpersonal relationships. The rationale behind this behavior stems from the inability of individuals whom you hold in high regard to acknowledge your worth, causing you to believe that your self-esteem is contingent upon circumstances beyond your control. Consequently, when these circumstances do not align with your expectations, you experience feelings of failure. Additionally, certain psychological conditions such as personality disorders and depression contribute to this phenomenon.

Engage in self-dialogue as if addressing a young child

I had been eagerly anticipating the football game for the entire week. I aspired to assume the role of the star player due to my exceptional performance as a center back.

I anticipated it to be a formidable endeavor given that our opponents were leading the league.

The match was contested, and my team emerged with a resounding 10-1 loss. That can be a common occurrence in youth football, unfortunately. My team had a modest standing in the middle of the league, however on occasion, they would suffer decisive defeats. I did not perform at my best level, and it was an immense source of embarrassment to me as I struggled to contain the attackers who mercilessly dominated the game.

It can be concluded that my internal dialogue was rather weak during this period.

Upon returning home from the game, I reacted abruptly when my exceptional mother posed a highly reasonable query. In an instant, the overwhelming sense of remorse for my impulsive outburst towards my mother brought forth an immediate flood of tears. I recognized her lack of deservingness, yet I acknowledged that it originated from the detrimental, merciless self-criticisms I inflicted upon myself.

"Useless footballer!"

"Pathetic!"

"Embarrassment!"

The profound wrath, vexation, and acute sense of inadequacy that plagued me for the majority of my existence whenever a misfortune occurred.

My exceptionally admirable and extraordinary Mother, the remarkable individual she is, observed this facet within me and embraced me. She knew me well.

This is not the solitary instance in my life that comes to mind. I am not the sole individual who harbors such thoughts or engages in self-criticism. When our tone of communication with young children mirrors the one we adopt towards ourselves, it is highly likely that they would respond with tears. Curiously, this mirrors the manner in which we treat ourselves when we exhibit an absence of compassion or fail to cultivate self-love. I was provided with an excellent elucidation of this psychological concept during my participation in a workshop focused on communication skills and professional presence. Additionally, a corroborating endorsement of this concept can be found in another recently read publication authored by esteemed confidence coach and human behavior specialist Jo Emerson, entitled "Flying for Beginners." Jo asserts the existence of an inner child, a youthful manifestation within our consciousness, which becomes evident as we engage in self-dialogue laden with disparaging remarks. In that case, it is akin to engaging in conversation with a younger iteration of ourselves, specifically one who is three years of age.

Additionally, I had the privilege of participating in an exceptionally enlightening spiritual psychology workshop titled 'Awaken' led by Allan

Kleynhans. I highly commend you to consider exploring his expertise as he possesses exceptional speaking skills and coaching abilities. Additionally, he serves as a trainer for Tony Robbins. During the workshop, he assisted several individuals who had concealed traumatic experiences in navigating their way through the healing process in order to rediscover the feeling of joy. I was able to witness the progression of their emotional suffering towards achieving liberation.

In order to genuinely embrace self-love, we require this. I have required this experience in order to reconnect with my inner child and provide self-care. We must endure the discomfort in order to foster a deeper love for ourselves.

Upon further reflection, it became evident to me that this line of reasoning was highly logical. There existed a small juvenile boy within my thoughts who had experienced the loss of his sibling and displayed a measure of bewilderment.

I was addressing him in an extremely disrespectful manner, resorting to using derogatory language towards him. Upon my initial attempt at engaging in that particular meditation practice, I underwent a profound emotional experience, wherein tears spontaneously welled up within me, despite being twenty-eight years of age at the time. Nevertheless, this occurrence instilled an unparalleled sense of solace within me, making it a truly transformative experience. I promptly commenced expressing remorse for the manner in which I had been engaging in self-dialogue.

Naturally, I encountered a few obstacles subsequent to that training session; however, upon implementing the practice of engaging in positive and compassionate self-talk, a significant improvement in my well-being ensued.

I have recently embraced a more spontaneous approach to life, finding joy in embracing a childlike mindset while still fulfilling my obligations as an adult.

Therefore, I kindly request that if you engage in self-deprecating self-talk, as I have for an extended period of time, please take a moment to reflect and consider. Envision a youthful incarnation of yourself residing within the depths of your being. Make it a priority to care for that individual and when you catch yourself engaging in self-criticism... pause and reflect: 'would I utter such hurtful statements to a toddler?'

In order to cultivate a more benevolent and empathetic internal dialogue, it is advisable to engage in regular and consistent self-communication, rather than solely reserving it for moments of distress. Once more, by consistently engaging in positive self-talk, the self-esteem muscle will undoubtedly strengthen. Put forth a deliberate effort to consciously reprogram the influx of negative thoughts.

Furthermore, on one occasion, my confidence coach imparted upon me invaluable guidance pertaining to the concept of the inner child and the importance of acceptance. Consider the scenario whereby you are bestowed with the responsibility of caring for a child, but rather than embracing this role, you persistently overlook their needs or subject them to criticism and fixate excessively on future circumstances. How would it feel? Should you refuse to acknowledge the current circumstances and disregard the nurturing of your inner child, the dormant inner child within you will begin to stir assertively.

Action:

One recommended practice entails writing in a journal for a brief duration of 2 or 3 minutes each morning or evening, outlining one's accomplishments from the preceding day and noting five positive attributes or qualities about oneself.

The second approach involves dedicating one minute each day to engaging in positive self-affirmation while looking into the mirror.

One additional suggestion is to envision engaging in conversation with your younger self at the age of three. Show empathy and goodwill, and envision this dialogue.

Naturally, there may be occasional obstacles (I will elaborate on a contingency plan later) but by consistently engaging in positive self-dialogue, you are cultivating a more constructive internal narrative that benefits your self-esteem.

Consistent Self-Improvement Is Paramount In Achieving Success.

So, it appears that you have enhanced your self-confidence. You have experienced personal growth and advancement through the use of positive self-reinforcement. If necessary, you have engaged in therapeutic sessions and made progress in cultivating a positive mindset, and it is now opportune to acquire the knowledge and skills to sustain this developmental trajectory.

Maintaining a positive mindset and adopting a positive outlook necessitate a daily decision. It is not an immediate occurrence, nor does it transpire without unwavering persistence. Developing and enhancing one's self-esteem and personal growth does not constitute a mere talent. It is a choice.

The objective at present is to construct and cultivate your self-esteem methodically. Your objective should be to continually expand, maintain a positive outlook, and express gratitude. The higher the level of positivity you maintain, the greater the likelihood of experiencing an amplification in your self-esteem.

Keep Growing

In order to keep your self-esteem growing and heading toward self-improvement, you have to keep growing and developing. The expansion must transpire within the domains of assuming personal responsibility for one's actions, identity, and conduct. As one cultivates an increased sense of self-worth, a corresponding growth in self-assurance, conscientiousness, and ethical principles becomes apparent.

What you are currently in pursuit of is personal development. You aspire to dedicate yourself to ongoing personal development, with a focus on enhancing your self-assurance. This is an objective that requires a daily commitment on your part. There may be obstacles and deviations along the path, yet rest assured that you are gradually developing into the individual you aspire to become and have the potential to be.

There are several strategies that can contribute to one's continuous growth, such as:

• Assess your strengths and areas for improvement and strive to achieve a harmonious work-life equilibrium.

• Facilitating the utilization of the advancements you have achieved in self-esteem and self-assurance in order to set yourself on the appropriate path and unveil the apt opportunities for further personal development.

• Please bear in mind that the process of personal growth and development holds significant importance in one's life.

• The greater self-awareness one possesses, the more one can cultivate their self-confidence.

Do not bother yourself about trivial matters; they are inconsequential.

In the year 1997, the author Richard Carlson penned the book titled 'Do Not Allow Minor Matters to Worry You... They Are All Trivial Matters'. In this literary work, Carlson observed individuals in a state of hurried activity and anxiety. He believed that a considerable number of individuals dedicated their lives to superfluous stress. He had a tendency to express that traffic remained indifferent and unconcerned towards one's state of stress.

Therefore, instead of experiencing stress, shift your attention towards cultivating a sense of gratitude. It is imperative to bear in mind the importance of exhibiting gratitude on a daily basis. Engaging in the act of showing appreciation will facilitate the development of your capacity to alleviate stress, particularly stress associated with trivial matters.

It is acceptable to experience fear - proceed with the task you believe you are incapable of doing.

While advocating for women to assert themselves, assume greater agency over their lives, contribute to societal progress, and assert their entitlement to equal rights alongside men, Eleanor Roosevelt proclaimed, "In the presence of apprehension, one must engage in the very endeavor they deem impossible."

Engage in activities that you perceive yourself incapable of. Embrace the challenge that instills the greatest fear within you and appears insurmountable. Have courage. It elicits a higher level of exhilaration compared to fear. Courage according to Mrs. "Roosevelt evokes greater exhilaration than fear, and ultimately, it proves to be less arduous." Mrs. Roosevelt delivered his speech prior to the onset of the Second World War, imparting a call-to-action for individuals to abandon apprehension and embrace courage. The greater the number of experiences one endures, the greater one's capacity to endure.

For Mrs. In reference to individuals grappling with the task of enhancing their self-esteem, the true peril resides in passivity, in evading one's apprehensions. For individuals who experience diminished self-confidence, confronting their fears may present an overwhelming challenge due to the apprehension of potential failure leading to further loss of self-assurance. Due to this, it is imperative that you achieve success with every attempt. It is imperative that you undertake the task you believe to be beyond your capabilities.

Learn from your Mistakes

The ultimate component of this fifth step, focusing on the ongoing enhancement of oneself, entails acquiring knowledge from one's past errors. You are now capable of accomplishing this, given the substantial personal growth you have achieved through your diligent efforts towards enhancing self-esteem.

You can gain valuable lessons from mistakes, regardless of their magnitude or insignificance. Allocate sufficient time for comprehensive analysis of the events, your actions, and alternative approaches that could be employed to yield a distinct result. The objective is not to merely compensate for your error, but rather to prevent its recurrence in the future and adapt your actions based on the lessons learned from this mistake.

Chapter Eleven: Cultivate Self-Assurance as a Regular Practice

Allow me to clarify a crucial point in this matter. I would like to convey to you the notion that individuals who possess confidence that appears to come naturally or effortlessly are not innately predisposed to possess such characteristics. Although there exists a minute subset of individuals who possess a genetic inclination towards positivity, optimism, and confidence, they comprise only a minority. The overwhelming majority of individuals who possess inherent confidence have acquired this attribute through the process of learning. Understand this. The presence of low self-confidence is not an inevitable outcome for you. If they are capable of achieving it, you also possess the ability to accomplish the same. This may appear to be intrinsic and instinctive to them, as they have assimilated confidence into their routine. You have the ability to accomplish it, too.

How do Habits work?

So, how can one cultivate self-confidence as a regular practice? First and foremost, it is imperative to determine the underlying mechanisms of patterns. Habits consist of three components.

There exists a stimulus or an indicator. This could potentially function as a social context. This can be words. This can be actions carried out by individuals other than oneself. This phenomenon may involve numerous external stimuli. Numerous diverse external stimuli can serve as cues.

The subsequent segment pertains to actions of a formal nature. There is no need for any further elucidation on this matter. Upon experiencing a trigger, you proceed to undertake the prescribed formal course of action. You experience an innate sense of obligation to engage in such behavior. Why? Due to the fact that you are in search of the third element.

The third component entails the execution of an action, which subsequently yields a favorable outcome or reward. This is the method by which one cultivates a habit. Many individuals tend to indulge in cigarette consumption immediately following a substantial meal. The stimulus is the sensation of satiety that individuals experience from their consumption. This is the stimulus that motivates them to retrieve their pack of cigarettes and ignite it. That action is customary. They identify the activation mechanism, and the recurrent action entails lighting one. Now, what is the desired outcome they seek? An additional benefit is that the presence of nicotine in their system induces vasoconstriction, enabling it to synergize with their brain chemistry and amplify the sensations of comfort and well-being derived from the recently consumed food. That represents the sought-after compensation.

Please note that habits consistently consist of three key components: the cue, the behavioral response, and the reward. Individuals who possess self-assurance can effectively utilize this system, irrespective of whether it is done deliberately or automatically, as it enables them to consistently maintain a state of unwavering certainty.

Individuals who possess confidence behave in a confident manner due to engrained practice.

What is the outcome or progression of this situation? In instances where a person recognizes the need for self-assurance, they employ techniques to ensure they exude confidence. Initially, this requires a certain degree of exertion. Once individuals become acclimated to the task, it becomes ingrained in their routine, leading to a sense of assurance and enabling them to proceed with confidence. When individuals approach their work with optimism, it yields positive outcomes.

Chapter 5

It all resides within the confines of our consciousness.

Direct your attention towards the positive aspects.

Collectively, we all encounter certain challenging circumstances in life as a natural part of the human experience.

It is typically not an opulent scenario. Ultimately, life is shaped by one's actions and attitudes

Maintaining a positive outlook despite unfavorable circumstances can make a significant impact.

and helps you navigate through challenging circumstances with a positive attitude.

Notwithstanding, the primary concern revolves around how one can maintain a positive outlook despite challenging circumstances.

Is it challenging to come? Maintaining a cheerful disposition in situations like this is the paramount priority.

While your thoughts should certainly take precedence, it is imperative that you approach the situation with a resolute mindset.

fore. "In order to maintain a positive mindset, it is essential to divert one's attention away from personal problems and concerns and instead re

Enhancing cognitive function becomes especially evident during challenging days when one is experiencing distress.

I am experiencing a sense of frustration with myself and have an inclination to retreat and express my emotions through tears. "Here are some exceptional suggestions for

Maintaining a perspective of inspiration in life, regardless of the challenges that surround you.

• If you find yourself surrounded by individuals who maintain a negative outlook, then free yourself from their company.

Cynicism possesses the ability to spread from one individual to another, as it cascades.

Are you in agreement or alignment with them?

• It is ill-advised to sit in front of the television for extended periods of time, as the content of the news may be distressing.

Encouragingly, police stations emphasize the prevalence of hostility, transience, and conflict in various iterations is evident in almost every television program. If you happen to watch television,

A suitable example of a more affirmative program could be a natural exposition that showcases the magnificent

The world in all its splendor or as a satirical imitation.

• Devote ample time to nurturing relationships with your loved ones and accomplishing your goals. • Prioritize quality time with your family and friends, while also fulfilling your responsibilities. • Make a conscious effort to dedicate considerable time to bonding with your family and friends, as well as achieving your objectives. • Maximize the amount of time you invest in cultivating meaningful connections with your family and friends, and completing tasks successfully.

Create an activity that everyone in the family enjoys and arrange for a collective evening dedicated to spending quality time together.

Experience a frequency of one occurrence per week, allowing for opportunities to socialize.

During moments of heightened emotional distress and the onset of skepticism, avail yourself of the opportunity to engage with

Listen to a motivational audio recording or consistently repeat affirmative affirmations in order to restore a sense of encouragement.

frame of mind.

• Allocate time each day to engage in an activity that you derive value and satisfaction from.

Does not anticipate you to make commitments or choices, thereby promoting a state of relaxation.

without limit.

• Attempt to achieve something outside of your usual routine, a task that is unquestionably

It is unconventional for you and deviates from the norm. Consider engaging in an alternative recreational pursuit or game that you may enjoy.

I have never yearned to engage in.

• Engage in physical activity, such as taking a leisurely walk in the fresh air.

Furthermore, it is completely unrestricted to either visit the recreational center or engage in activities such as yoga.

ga.

- Establish personal goals that will enable you to surpass expectations, and upon successfully attaining each goal, affirm your accomplishments

insignificant recompense for undertaking such actions.

- Acquire techniques that facilitate the redirection of your attention and focus

Swiftly completing a nearby task.

- Employ affirmations throughout the day to cultivate self-assurance and optimism

contemplations and emotions.

- It is imperative to consistently seek out the positive aspects in challenging situations, even though the outcomes may not align with our expectations.

We anticipate that upon thorough investigation, one may uncover that they do not possess the assumed qualities.

Despite their seemingly appalling nature.

• Please be mindful of the fact that this situation is not permanent and is merely a passing phase that you are currently undergoing. Rest assured, it will eventually improve.

The possibilities are boundless for you.

You have the potential to accomplish anything upon which you direct your unwavering concentration. The possibilities are boundless, and limitations are merely a threshold to surpass.

By undertaking a series of fundamental steps, one can accomplish anything in life. The

The optimal method for making progress predominantly involves unwavering dedication to achieving your desired objectives, while adhering to established guidelines."

Direct your efforts towards taking the necessary steps to accomplish your goals and adapt accordingly.

Adhere to the prescribed methodology and persist with this novel approach until you achieve your desired outcome. The means

are relatively straightforward to pursue and modifications can be easily implemented to determine your accommodation

To properly address any task or objective in various facets of life, let us now examine the aforementioned steps.

Commitment

It is imperative that you take proactive action and carefully determine your objectives in order to achieve desired outcomes.

"Immerse yourself in the everyday course of life and establish a clear aim. Once your mind is focused on your desired outcome,

One should approach it with unwavering conviction and a sense of solemn obligation. During the process of organizing and preparing

When determining your objective, it is essential to possess unwavering conviction in achieving it, regardless of the obstacles. Envisioning your objective holistically, from its initiation to its fruition, and picturing yourself successfully attaining whatever you aspire to accomplish is imperative.

Engage in the necessary measures" "Undertake whatever actions are necessary" "Exert efforts to achieve the required results" "Implement any necessary courses of action" "Ensure all requisite steps are taken

When you have made the conscious decision to go all out and accept the responsibility, then the sub

The next step entails initiating progress towards your goal, taking tangible actions to move forward.

The most challenging aspect, as it necessitates venturing into the outside world and genuinely achieving substantial outcomes.

Contemplating the actions required and expressing your unwavering commitment to accomplishing them is relatively straightforward, nonetheless

Implementing strategies to address the unknown and approaching your plan with enthusiasm.

The stage often becomes a stumbling block for many individuals, as fear inhibits their progress.

Sticking with it

When you have made the decision and embarked on the pursuit of your vision or aspiration,

In order to make an objective a reality, it is essential to exhibit perseverance and a willingness to adapt methodologies until a successful outcome is achieved.

Ultimately, reach your desired goal. Depending on your choice of action,

It is imperative that you allocate sufficient time, while maintaining a steadfast focus on managing the task at hand.

By starting anew, it can meticulously record the chronicles of your endeavor from initiation to culmination.

By considering these factors, you can ascertain the extent of your progress and maintain your focus.

the desired outcome you intend to achieve. Life is replete with various unexpected idiosyncrasies and has the ability to throw any unforeseen challenges our way.

It is imperative that you continue to push yourself forward in the face of any unexpected challenges, as they carry great importance.

The journeys persist relentlessly towards the desired outcome. Over time, fear becomes the primary concern and the primary factor behind the failure of most individuals.

achieve and relinquish their intended goals, if you succumb to apprehension it shall

Continually endeavor to arrange larger squares in your chosen fashion until eventually they overpower you and compel your surrender.

The possibilities are truly limitless if you embark on a journey with unwavering perseverance and determination to overcome any obstacle that comes your way.

Negative Thoughts Contribute to the Development of Negative Individuals

The presence of pessimistic thoughts in one's mind inevitably leads to the manifestation of a negative disposition, leaving no room for uncertainty in this matter. The perception of pessimism can be swiftly detected by individuals in their interactions with others. If you perceive the individual with whom you are engaging as being inclined towards pessimism, there is likely a valid justification for this perception. While they may contend that they are merely adopting a pragmatic perspective, it serves as a rationalization for their prevailing negative outlook at that particular moment.

Ultimately, individuals harboring a pessimistic mindset are often those who are grappling with personal challenges and tend to perceive situations in an unfavorable light. They are merely performing perfunctory actions, repeatedly succumbing to the influx of negativity in their lives, which inundates them and dictates their every move, every word they utter, and their purpose for being or engaging with the world. This is a significant issue that often arises; it is important to acknowledge that individuals with a negative mindset are likely burdened by such thoughts and will require a transformation. In the upcoming chapter, we will shortly delve into the manifestations and repercussions of negative thinking and the presence of negativity. In the initial segment, we shall be elucidating the prevailing cognitive patterns and their potential impact on both interpersonal dynamics and cognitive processes.

It is important to acknowledge that negativity is detrimental to one's well-being. It will not yield any advantageous outcomes for you. It will not facilitate your ability to effectively engage with the world. It will not aid in determining the utmost significance in life. It will not contribute to your sense of achievement or progress. Conversely, it will cause a decline in your progress. You will be miserable. You will be unhappy. One may encounter difficulties in engaging with others and may experience a sense of personal melancholy as a result of the relationships and interactions encountered. It is imperative that you acquire the knowledge and understanding necessary to overcome this obstacle and emerge victorious from the clutches of negativity.

Nevertheless, prior to conquering the pessimism, one must initially acknowledge its existence. It is crucial to acquire the skills to effectively perceive and comprehend the manner in which your interactions with the world unfold, in order to enhance your ability to adapt and navigate through it proficiently. Only when one attains the capacity to comprehend their actions, thought processes, and the underlying causes of their prevailing thoughts, are they truly capable of initiating genuine and substantial advancement towards the attainment of positivity in their life, which is an essential prerequisite for achieving success.

Do you possess a pessimistic disposition?

Ultimately, you may possess a pessimistic disposition. You may not have come to this realization yet, or you may have already discerned it simply from perusing the aforementioned list. It is conceivable that one might come to the realization of possessing a negative outlook on life, should they find themselves able to personally identify with a multitude of such divergent perspectives.

In order to ascertain whether one possesses a propensity for negativity, it becomes imperative to engage in introspective contemplation. How frequently do you find yourself hindered by sentiments of pessimism? To what extent do you frequently encounter circumstances where your emotions hinder your progress? Can you establish a connection with the list that has just been provided to you? How frequently do you experience such sentiments?

Once more, it is important to bear in mind that a certain degree of negativity is a natural and beneficial aspect of life. It occurs periodically, and there is no cause for embarrassment. That is an occurrence that sporadically takes place, and you will be fully justified in acknowledging and cooperating with it. You can readily attain reconciliation with that perspective as long as you maintain a commendable equilibrium between optimistic and pessimistic thoughts.

It might come as a revelation, but in broader terms, embodying a positive disposition entails maintaining a state of mind wherein approximately 80% of one's thoughts are positive in nature. In other words, if you find yourself focusing on negative thoughts about 20% of the time, you can consider yourself a positive individual, as you have been granted a 4:1 ratio of positive to negative thoughts. Nevertheless, should you discover an abundance of negative thoughts surpassing the mentioned threshold, or if you observe a balanced proportion between positive and negative thoughts, it is plausible to conclude that you are indeed inclined towards negativity, leaving no room for dispute on this matter. Fortunately, nevertheless, by recognizing and overcoming those pessimistic thoughts, you will discover that acquiring the ability to cultivate a positive mindset, which you have long aspired to achieve, is indeed attainable.

What are the Detrimental Effects of Negativity on Your Well-being?

Engaging with negativity tends to foster a melancholic disposition. It engenders a negative temperament, thereby regrettably impacting your overall well-being.

Adverse energy possesses the potential to dismantle and impact familial bonds, friendships, and interpersonal connections.

The presence of negativity has the potential to elicit anger, and it is common knowledge that anger can lead to impulsive actions that may be remorseful in hindsight.

Negativity affects your brain. According to health professionals, prolonged contemplation of negative thoughts, even for a mere thirty minutes, may lead to the degeneration of neurons within the neurocampus region of the brain, thereby compromising one's cognitive abilities related to problem-solving.

Primarily, the issue with engaging in negative thinking is its overall lack of productivity. If it fails to achieve any tangible results and neglects to acknowledge the root cause, it will not facilitate the cultivation of behaviors that are genuinely productive or supportive of success. When one succumbs to the influence of negativity, one shall find oneself in a state of profound discontent. Furthermore, just as negativity has the potential to proliferate within one's own thoughts, it possesses the capacity to be transmitted to others as well. Indeed, it is common advice for individuals to sever all ties with negative individuals in order to cease the perpetuation of negativity and safeguard themselves from internalizing and subsequently manifesting such negativity.

Engaging in pessimistic thoughts will not facilitate the resolution of your difficulties. Pessimistic thoughts only serve to hinder one's progress. If one truly believes that their efforts are unlikely to yield any solution to the current predicament, why would they invest their time and energy in attempting to address it? Viewed as a mere drain on their limited and valuable energy, the attempts would be perceived as futile and unworthy of pursuit. It is improbable that you would do so, as you would instead opt to redirect your efforts towards a more practical and feasible approach in order to achieve the desired outcome. Regrettably, individuals harboring a despondent outlook, pervaded by pessimism, are unlikely to perceive everything as deserving of such attentiveness and exertion. Instead, you will likely choose to continue being inactive.

Naturally, the ultimate outcome consequently leads to the counterproductive conviction that it lacks value since no transformations will occur. If one fails to actively contribute towards the desired transformation, it is only natural that no alteration will occur. There will inevitably be ongoing discontent that arises purely as a result of your actions. Consider it from this perspective: when attempting to address an issue, there exists the potential for improvement to occur. Nonetheless, should one refrain from attempting, the probability of encountering failure will inevitably reach 100%. One cannot ascertain the impossibility or the predetermined outcome of events without making any attempts or undertaking any risks.

Consider the following perspective - your prevailing belief is that you lack value. You convince yourself that you are unable to achieve success in your professional endeavors due to your perceived lack of value. As a result of holding that conviction, you refrain from submitting an application for the aforementioned job, a position in which you possess considerable aptitude. Consequently, by neglecting to pursue the opportunity, you forfeit the chance to substantiate your competence in the professional setting. Your conviction that you will never attain the requisite competence for any employment opportunity has hindered your ability to secure a position, thereby perpetuating the relentless circle of pessimism.

Conversely, your pessimistic thoughts might manifest themselves at a later point, thereby highlighting and reinforcing the beliefs you have steadfastly clung to. As an illustration, should one hold the belief of personal worthlessness and subsequently encounter rejection when applying for employment, one may deem this particular occurrence as substantiation for the aforementioned pessimistic mindset. You reassure yourself that, undoubtedly, you were unsuccessful in securing the position; you perceive yourself as lacking value. Given that you were not offered the position, it is understandable that you may find further validation for the negative thoughts you currently hold. One might tend to attribute their failure in the job to their own actions, or convince themselves that they can never achieve success like their peers, resulting in difficulty in finding motivation to continue or make further attempts. Consequently, this reinforces the cycle of adopting self-defeating and pessimistic beliefs.

Listen Keenly

Developing excellent listening skills is a crucial endeavor that can prove to be immensely challenging for many individuals. It can be challenging to attentively listen, particularly when simultaneously grappling with personal matters. In order to establish effective rapport or improve interpersonal connections, active listening is imperative.

Active listening enables one to perceive auditory stimuli, facilitating comprehension of the other party's perspective and their worldview. Engaging in active listening, a technique that involves restating the person's words once they have been expressed, enables one to establish a meaningful rapport with the individual in question.

By actively listening, one can empathize with others by adopting their perspective, leading to a deeper comprehension of their thoughts and feelings.

Exercise Caution in Interpreting Non-verbal Signals

Psychologists have posited that nonverbal communication often imparts more information than verbal communication. However, it is advisable to refrain from excessive speculation on the veracity of this claim and redirect our focus towards a scenario in which we encounter difficulty in effectively articulating our thoughts and feelings orally. What activities do you frequently engage in?

When you are in a crowded environment, anticipating the arrival of someone, you might unconsciously display your restlessness by rhythmically tapping an object, such as a table or the armrest of your chair. Alternatively, when experiencing anxiety and restlessness, one might engage in the act of manipulating objects in their hands.

Frequently, we unknowingly emit these signals. Hence, even when we articulate something that is incongruent with our emotional state, our nonverbal communication has the potential to expose our true feelings.

Therefore, in order to enhance your social awareness, it is essential to be observant of the unspoken messages conveyed by individuals. Observe their demeanor outside of verbal communication. Observe their behavior when they are unable to communicate verbally. Acquiring the skills to decipher these signals will enhance your ability to modify your communication to align with their present emotional state. Therefore, you will endeavor to ease the tension of the apprehensive individual, perhaps through the utilization of humor, prior to advancing your argument.

Demonstrating a pronounced level of attentiveness towards individuals' conduct during social exchanges will establish an impression that you hold them and their expressions in high regard. This realization will assist you in establishing a connection more quickly with them. Nevertheless, it is imperative to bear in mind that executing this task with great skill is crucial, as any lack of care may result in conveying an unsettling impression. The crucial factor lies in being attentive to their non-verbal signals and engaging with them in a manner that elicits a response contrary to their initial reaction, all while ensuring that they do not feel under scrutiny.

Be Empathetic

Exhibiting empathy serves as the utmost pivotal means to establish rapport. In order to cultivate a sense of compassion, it is imperative to attain self-awareness first and foremost.

However, attaining proficiency in empathy proves to be a challenging endeavor. Due to our conviction in the exceptional nature of our existence and concepts, practicing empathy entails observing individuals with a recognition of their inherent humanity. Empathy entails making a sincere effort to understand the perspectives of others and engage with them accordingly. It may prove more challenging in practice.

On how many occasions have you encountered the puzzlement of comprehending an individual's rationale behind their beliefs? To what extent have you frequently formed conclusive evaluations of individuals without affording yourself the opportunity to gain insight into their perspective?

Frequently, we tend to commit this oversight on numerous occasions, thereby highlighting the importance of cultivating empathy.

To exhibit empathy is to recognize and honor the inherent humanity of the individual, even in instances where our perspectives diverge. It indicates that you recognize the possibility that the individual who displayed rudeness towards you might have been burdened by their personal challenges. It signifies that you possess a comprehension of the rationale behind another individual's seemingly irrational and imprudent choice.

Granting others the space to exhibit their humanity and make mistakes is a fundamental aspect of emotional development and cognitive acumen. Subsequently, it implies that within your interpersonal dealings, you will exhibit a greater inclination to actively listen to others, express agreement, and deliberate without demeaning them. Being empathetic is crucial in valuing your friendships and fulfilling your role, as it entails comprehending the innate human desire for affection and acknowledgment, which is commonly known as the principle of esteem.

Therefore, it is advisable to exercise empathy during your interactions with others. To initiate the conversation, when engaging with individuals and encountering divergent perspectives, it is advisable to refrain from interjecting one's own beliefs and instead inquire about their worldview. After acquiring knowledge about these individuals, one can employ persuasive techniques in order to encourage them to adopt an alternative viewpoint.

This practice will undoubtedly pose challenges in circumstances where the matter in question evokes strong emotions and creates widespread disagreement. It becomes increasingly challenging to cultivate empathy towards the other person, particularly when they exhibit a determined inclination to adhere to their own beliefs.

At this juncture, it is essential to put into practice the preceding lesson on conflict management by discerning the optimal moment to disengage or minimize further losses. It is not possible to alter an individual's entrenched ignorance through empathetic means. In the event that it appears they are not offering you the same level of attentive listening as you provide them, it may be best to disengage, for the reason that emotional intelligence also encompasses recognizing when it is appropriate to discontinue the interaction.

Effectively manage and direct one's emotions."

To regulate one's emotions does not imply a suppression or deprivation of these emotional experiences. Additionally, there are alternative means through which you can articulate those thoughts.

According to the assertion made by Mark Manson, it is stated that one's emotions are beyond control, however, the pivotal factor lies in how one chooses to respond to their thoughts.

Intense emotions possess the capacity to restructure the neural pathways within our brains. They exhibit disruptive behavior and lead to a state of imbalance for us. As we embark on the journey of enhancing our emotional intelligence, it is prudent for me to refrain from discussing negative emotions. Nonetheless, we have witnessed the potentially devastating consequences that they can bring about. Furthermore, it is worth noting that even positive emotions such as joy or happiness can have significant impacts. When emotions are aroused within us, consequential shifts in our body's chemical reactions occur, giving rise to a range of physical and psychological alterations. Consequently, our attention becomes intensively directed towards the individual or occurrence that is responsible for our elation, contentment, or agitation.

And to experience emotional states is to be inherently vulnerable to a myriad of human achievements. Upon exploring the archives of our history, it becomes apparent that individuals frequently harnessed their emotions to create works of art, literature, or spearhead social movements. Consider the manner in which individuals who experienced profound sorrow and a profound sense of deprivation would historically initiate collective actions. We can examine the actions taken by mothers who have experienced substantial harm in order to tackle the problem that led to their tragedy, such as the organization Mothers Against Drunken Driving.

Upon analyzing anger, it is perceived as a detrimental emotional state. And it is true. Rage is an intense emotion that we can manage effectively, enhancing our quality of life. Furthermore, we can observe how the utilization of passion enables us to perform impeccably. Human rights movements and various social change movements frequently consist of individuals who have become disillusioned with the existing state of affairs, thus channeling their dissatisfaction towards amplifying their voices.

As you embark on the journey of cultivating greater self-awareness, you will come to recognize that amidst each emotional tumult you encounter, there exist avenues through which you can effectively harness its potential for positive transformation. Your sorrow may instill within you a heightened willingness to confront the circumstances that precipitated your bereavement. Your elation may prompt you to engage in a dialogue regarding the circumstances that caused your distress, in order to prevent recurrence. Rage has the potential to enhance concentration and propel societal transformation. All of these endeavors contribute to your increased societal worth, even in the absence of acknowledgment or acclaim. The task is undertaken in order to enhance one's immediate environment.

This practice of directing our emotions towards productive endeavors is referred to as positive psychology, a discipline that urges us to not only cultivate and embrace our positive emotions, but also to acknowledge and accept our negative emotions. They have a purpose, namely that negative emotions serve as powerful catalysts for change, in greater measure than positive emotions do.

Consequently, what steps can be taken to effectively redirect and harness the emotions in a more beneficial manner?

#18 Act in accordance with ethical principles

Have you neglected any necessary tasks that remain unfinished in your list of responsibilities? Are you procrastinating? Engaging in actions aligned with one's inner convictions serves to bolster one's confidence and self-regard. Engage in tasks that you have been procrastinating, such as attending the forthcoming familial gathering, engaging in physical exercise, practicing forgiveness towards others, obtaining your driver's license, and other similar endeavors.

When you act in accordance with moral principles, not only will you attain favorable outcomes, but you will also experience a sense of personal satisfaction.

"#19 Respond to errors and setbacks in a more productive manner

Experiencing failure or committing errors is not unique to your circumstances. Each one of us experiences failure in varying degrees, some of which can be quite remarkable. However, these individuals exhibit resilience by refusing to allow such failures to dictate their sense of self-value. What distinguishes your failures in such a manner that they assume a position of (dis)repute in your personal journey? Perceive them as they truly are, merely errors and not pivotal events or momentous incidents of great magnitude. And they are now in the past, concluded.

The most optimal course of action with regard to these experiences is to let go of them and derive valuable lessons from them. Do not excessively criticize or blame yourself for that minor lapse. Those individuals whom you believe are still evaluating you based on that error have likely forgotten what transpired or whether it even took place. When faced with adversity, endeavor to uplift and encourage yourself, employing the same compassionate approach one would extend to a cherished companion. Indeed, if you are indeed a true friend, it is expected that you will provide solace, upliftment, strategize methods to mitigate the consequences, and even discern silver linings in the face of an error. Apply the same actions or treatment to yourself.

#20 Be assertive

Advocate for yourself, assert your desires and uphold your principles. If you truly deem it appropriate, avail yourself of the liberty to alter your standpoint. Your assertiveness appears to be lacking when you acquiesce to the desires of others at your own detriment, allow yourself to be subjected to bullying or condescending behavior, or struggle to express your needs or claim what is rightfully yours. Thus, what measures can be taken to enhance one's assertiveness?

*Practice saying No firmly

Acquire awareness of the non-verbal signals you emit when experiencing a sense of inadequacy and refrain from displaying them, such as engaging in restless movements.

Maintain your resolve when confronted with aggression and promptly confront the aggressive conduct.

Acquire the skills of assertiveness through participation in a comprehensive training program, by closely observing assertive conduct, and by diligently engaging in practical exercises.

#8 Say No and mean it

Someone once stated that you must eliminate the habit of attempting to please everyone all the time if you want to be truly confident. Why even consider trying to accomplish it when it is impossible? When you agree to something you don't want to do, your stress levels go up, your self-confidence goes down, and you feel more insignificant. People who are confident don't feel obligated to comply with requests. They are not required to comply just because someone requests their opinion if doing so causes them inconvenience. How can you be certain that you are skilled in saying no?

*Just say No, clearly and unambiguously

*Don't give excuses, apologies or justifications for saying No

*Give a good reason why you are turning down the request.

#9 Receiving and giving compliments

Accept compliments gracefully. Do not regard compliments with suspicions of an ulterior motive. When complimented, do not, for example, roll your eyes and say "Yeah, right" or shrug it off. Make sure you appreciate the compliment with a smile and a thank you, as this will make both the giver and you, the receiver feel good and build on your self-esteem. What to do when paying compliments:

*Be sincere-pay a compliment only when it is deserved

*Keep it short and sweet

*Avoid negative undertones e.g. "I never thought you could make such a powerful presentation"

*Avoid putting yourself down while complimenting e.g. "You look so great in that gown, I know I cannot look half as good".

#10 Handling Criticisms

Your self-confidence can be damaged by others' critical remarks since they seem to imply that you are unworthy or incapable. Do not let the criticism cause you to feel wounded or ashamed. Consider the criticism in its proper context; before responding, find out who is criticizing you and whether it is fair. Reject it with a firm no if it is unfair. *Recognize the criticism without expressing regret or providing an explanation, such as "You're correct, I did that. I appreciate you telling me. Any conflicts will end as a result.

*Ask incisive inquiries to ascertain the critic's grievances. This will transform the critique into an engaging conversation.

#11 Take a risk

Try something new, unknown and different. Get out of your comfort zone. When you do what is unexpected, you feel good about yourself. If you succeed, especially where you did not anticipate success, your confidence will surely sky-rocket. Push yourself and prove yourself;

stop avoiding new challenges and shying away from awkward situations or difficult people. Remember that confidence is a muscle that can only be built by constant practice. Even though it is prudent to take an inventory of your fears, do not overly dwell on them. Instead, adopt the motto; Feel the fear and do it anyway!

#12 Take care of your appearance

-Dress smartly. While it's true that a man is not defined by his clothes, looking nice affects how you conduct yourself, interact with others, and how they see you.

-Personal hygiene and grooming: Always appear presentable, tidy, well-groomed, and with neatly styled hair.

-Stand up straight, shoulders back, head up, and make eye contact to project a confident demeanor and make a good first impression.

Exercise regularly to stay in shape and feel better in both body and mind.

#13 Forgive and forget

Are you blaming others for the way you are or how your life turned out? It's time to get rid of the victim mentality and forgive. Make a list of all those whom you feel have hurt you; there will probably be any number of people including your parents, schoolteachers, ex-lovers. Resolve to truly forgive each one.

Remember that forgiving does not mean that you condone what was done, but that you are willing to live with whatever happened. It doesn't matter whether the perpetrators deserve forgiveness or not; what matters is that you are doing it for yourself, not for them. You are letting go of past hurts, bitterness and resentments that have pulled you down and cluttered your life.

You are creating room for new enriching experiences. You are becoming free.

Finally, do not forget to forgive yourself for all your past failings, for being too hard on yourself, for not standing up for yourself and for the hurts you have caused others.

-Dress smartly. While it's true that a man is not defined by his clothes, looking nice affects how you conduct yourself, interact with others, and how they see you.

-Personal hygiene and grooming: Always appear presentable, tidy, well-groomed, and with neatly styled hair.

-Stand up straight, shoulders back, head up, and make eye contact to project a confident demeanor and make a good first impression.

Exercise regularly to stay in shape and feel better in both body and mind.

Consider how you can utilize it more effectively, scenarios where you can use it more frequently, and what else you can do with your ability. Find the traits and skills you appreciate and would like to develop; examples include patience, empathy, meeting deadlines, offering guidance to problematic children, etc. Find out what it takes to obtain each attribute you've outlined, then strive resolutely toward doing so.

With every enhancement and achievement, your self-assurance will ascend to a higher level.

#15 Allocate additional time to engage with individuals who exhibit a positive and supportive influence.

Associate yourself with individuals who uplift and support you, rather than belittle or discourage you. May I inquire about the composition of your familial, social, and acquaintance networks? Could they serve as an exemplar in your endeavor to cultivate confidence? Do they exhibit happiness, confidence, assertiveness, kindness, and optimism? If so, keep them. If not, minimize the duration of your interactions with them or, if possible, endeavor to completely evade their company, as associating with them is likely to have a detrimental effect on you. It seems that the commonality between you and them has diminished.

Opt for engaging in literature or visual media that aligns with your pursuit of a heightened state of self-assurance. For instance, I have a fondness for perusing romantic literature, yet I conscientiously refrain from engaging with narratives that depict the female protagonist as feeble, reliant on rescue, and vastly inadequate compared to the male lead. I find the spirited, resilient, and intellectually astute protagonist particularly resonant.

#16 Treat others with kindness and respect.

Be kinder and helpful. There is an inherent sense of elevation that accompanies the act of actively assisting others, particularly individuals who are unfamiliar to us. Have you ever encountered the feeling of a profound upliftment in your state of being? It does not necessarily require grand gestures, but can instead encompass ordinary, everyday behaviors such as sincerely complimenting others, expressing gratitude, and refraining from mocking or belittling others. When one opts to enact a constructive transformation in the lives of others, they come to realize their role as a beneficial influence in society. This greatly enhances your level of self-assurance.

#17 Addressing and challenging erroneous or pessimistic thoughts

The perspectives you maintain regarding something may not encompass the sole means of perceiving it. Additionally, these thoughts may be imprecise. Examine these notions with thorough consideration of the information and reasoning at hand in order to ascertain their accuracy, subsequently disregarding any elements that prove to be incorrect or lacking in factual basis.

These perceptions or opinions may merely be exerting a constraining influence on you. Specifically, endeavor to refrain from:

*Drawing erroneous conclusions based on emotions- e.g. "Due to my unfortunate misstep and subsequent fall, I must conclude that I possess a certain level of clumsiness."

Engaging in unfavorable self-commentary, such as doubting my ability to successfully handle the situation

Formal alternative: "Formulating hasty negative assumptions without substantial evidence, such as inferring that 'my friend deliberately omitted my invitation to her party, implying that she perceives me as uninteresting'."

Transforming positives into negatives: exemplified by dismissing your accomplishments, asserting that they hold no significance, for instance, stating, 'I received this promotion solely due to the company's growth.'

Tools For Self-Awareness

Self-awareness is undoubtedly the cornerstone of emotional intelligence. In order to comprehend others, it is incumbent upon oneself to possess a profound comprehension of one's own being. Initially, one may engage in introspection by posing a series of inquiries to assess the quality of their self-awareness. Reflect upon your personal experiences and contemplate the adversities you have encountered throughout the course of your existence. Your narrative will elucidate your perception of your own life, thus unveiling the extent of your self-awareness. If your response leans towards uncertainty, such as, 'I am unable to ascertain as I experienced a relatively typical upbringing.' I consider myself fortunate to have secured my current position, but I remain uncertain about my prospects for the future. Nevertheless, the information provided will address any inquiries you may have.

You are an individual who has not fully assimilated their life narrative into their overall sense of self. One might find oneself devoid of purpose, direction, or comprehension regarding the motivations behind their actions.

A more introspective response could be articulated as follows: "I am a 32-year-old gentleman hailing from the Northwest region, who subsequently relocated to California for higher education." As an individual possessing exceptional proficiency and aptitude in programming, I was presented with a plethora of employment opportunities. After careful consideration, I made the deliberate choice to accept my current position due to its perceived status as the most advantageous alternative. I anticipate encountering a compatible individual with whom I can establish a stable and lasting relationship in the near future. The individual who provided this response exudes self-awareness and a clear sense of direction.

Regrettably, intentional acquisition of self-awareness is an unachievable endeavor. It is an attribute that accompanies the passage of time and accumulation of expertise, akin to sagacity. One can foster self-awareness by occasionally stepping outside of one's personal frameworks and actively engaging with unfamiliar experiences that challenge one's accustomed perspectives. As an illustration, if you have never experienced the opportunity to attend a recital of a particular genre of music, it would behoove you to sojourn in its sonic realm. Only then can you ascertain whether it resonates with your discerning sensibilities. This will provide you with context and comprehensive information regarding your music preferences, elucidating the reasons behind your inclination towards a particular genre while comparing it to alternative styles.

In various aspects, we occasionally develop a sense of complacency, which hinders our inclination for progress and transformation. This is a comprehensible aspect of human nature, yet it cannot serve as the basis upon which we proceed with our lives. We should endeavor to step out of our comfort zones. I am confident that you have encountered this on numerous occasions. The general population remains oblivious to the readily available opportunities beyond their comfort zone. Perhaps you could consider taking a leisurely trip downtown in the company of some friends, as the downtown area is located at a considerable distance, and typically you do not have the inclination to undertake such a lengthy drive. That is acceptable! You are capable of achieving it. Deviate from your customary routine and endeavor to partake in unfamiliar activities; this will enhance your self-awareness as it exposes you to new experiences that may expand your perspectives.

There are a multitude of activities that one can engage in to broaden their horizons and embrace novel experiences. You have the option to pursue a novel leisure activity, such as. Perhaps you have harbored a longstanding desire to acquire musical proficiency within a band setting. Acquiring an affordable instrument and leveraging online resources would facilitate an easily accessible entry into this hobby. This opportunity will afford you a fresh means of self-expression, along with intellectual activities that will support the agility and concentration of your mind.

One additional crucial aspect to consider in the analysis of individuals is having a comprehensive comprehension of behaviorism, specifically focusing on the intricate framework of the reward system in relation to the reinforcement and penalty of specific actions. Within the field of behaviorism, this practice is conducted in order to investigate the phenomenon of learning. Behaviorism has largely established that our learning is influenced by the application of rewards and punishments based on our behavior. When we receive recognition or reinforcement for our actions, be it the satisfaction of emotional release or physical pleasure, like indulging in a treat like candy, we tend to repeat the behavior on multiple occasions. When repercussions are associated with a specific action, our inclination to engage in said action will diminish, if feasible. This constitutes the primary essence of our acquisition as human and animal beings, and occasionally, its intricacies surpass initial perception. Take the activity of running, for instance, which elicits a distinct cerebral reward. During periods of physical exertion, such as running or engaging in strenuous activities, our brain releases certain chemicals that induce feelings of well-being. This notion may lead you to surmise that we possess an inherent inclination towards engaging in running and physical exertion, wouldn't it? Indeed, we possess an inherent inclination to be affected by external factors as well. As an example, the gratification derived from sugar consumption induces a profound sensation of pleasure, which can potentially give rise to addictive tendencies. Moreover, there is the anguish and challenge encountered while engaging in running while lacking optimal physical condition, thereby serving as a simultaneous penalization for partaking in the said activity. If an individual possesses the cognitive ability to recognize that engaging in running will entail certain discomfort but result in subsequent alleviation. They will grasp the means to engage in the endeavor and obtain the ultimate reward.

Certain states, such as persistent addiction, have the capacity to alter the functioning of the brain. The brain progressively becomes accustomed to repeated exposure to certain substances, such as sugar, fat, or the satisfaction derived from pornography, treating them as sources of reward. Nevertheless, over time, these reward centers become desensitized, impeding their ability to acknowledge the substances as sources of gratification.

Subsequently, the brain no longer regards the object of addiction as a form of reward. Nevertheless, the individual persistently participates in the endeavor repeatedly. The individual is entangled in a repetitive pattern whereby they remain driven to participate in the undertaking despite the absence of any further gratification. This is a frequently encountered state that numerous individuals experience with various substances and activities.

An essential competency in the endeavor of enhancing emotional intelligence involves comprehending the elements pertaining to one's early upbringing and familial background that have shaped their existence. This holds significant importance as the family of origin serves as the initial ground for the development of our methods of engaging with the world and existing within it. These individuals are the ones we aspire to resemble as we mature. They exemplify the concepts of masculinity and femininity that permeate our daily existence. Indeed, these are instances that exemplify all the behaviors which we comprehend initially. It is by viewing situations from this perspective that we are able to truly comprehend individuals' incentives, as human development does not occur in isolation. They are raised in the presence of fallible individuals who commit errors and exhibit unpredictability.

The skill of visual observation holds significant value in the application of emotional intelligence. Through visual observation, one gains the ability to meticulously examine body language and discern individuals' genuine intentions. Moreover, this aptitude facilitates the analysis of facial expressions, personal hygiene, attire, and various other visual indicators.

Proficiency in written communication is an additional fundamental characteristic associated with emotional intelligence. It would be advisable for you to commence documenting your observations of individuals whom you encounter in your daily life. Engaging in this activity will cultivate a perspective that influences your perception of the world. Initially, the voice may exhibit signs of apprehension or excessive presumption. However, this issue is adaptable, and initially, you may encounter uncertainty regarding its resolution. In due course, you shall become acclimated to your voice and acquire the skills necessary to effectively utilize it. Continuing to refine and cultivate your voice over time will ultimately result in its integration into your personal demeanor, extending its presence beyond the act of writing itself. What constitutes the nature of intuitional observation? We all possess it; we simply need to adapt to adhering to it.

Numerous individuals encounter difficulties in effectively adhering to their instinct. There could be several factors that lead individuals to doubt themselves, one of which is the belief that they lack the necessary competence to succeed in any endeavor. An additional factor could possibly be their perception of themselves as being unsuccessful. Regardless of the cause, it is imperative that you overcome this and commence placing trust in your intuition. Your intuition is a conceptual framework, with its essence lying in the discretion to rely on one's instincts. The term "trust" is frequently used in this context due to the necessity of having faith in one's own intuition, ensuring that it does not lead to misguided or erroneous conclusions, should such a possibility exist. As time progresses, as you acquire knowledge in heeding your intuition, you will experience a greater sense of reliance upon it, guiding you on the trajectory towards the attainment of self-realization.

The state of self-realization manifests when there exists a seamless unity between one's authentic self and the individual presented to the external world. Self-actualization occurs when one achieves full transparency and authenticity within oneself and in relation to the external world. This phenomenon occurs when comprehensive analysis of others is achievable, owing to the exhaustive exploration of every conceivable possibility within oneself. You possess ample expertise to discern the typical behavioral patterns of individuals in the midst of experiencing certain circumstances.

www.ingramcontent.com/pod-product-compliance
Lightning Source LLC
Chambersburg PA
CBHW050246120526
44590CB00016B/2232